Graphic Organizers in Science™

Learning About Energy with Graphic Organizers

Jonathan Kravetz

The Rosen Publishing Group's
PowerKids Press™
New York

For Sarah, my infinite source of energy

Published in 2007 by The Rosen Publishing Group, Inc.
29 East 21st Street, New York, NY 10010

First Edition

Editor: Jennifer Way
Layout Design: Julio A. Gil

Photo Credits: Cover, title page (center) © www.istockphoto.com/Sean McCarthy; cover, title page (top left), p. 7 (top center) © www.istockphoto.com/Christoph Ermel; cover, title page (top right), pp. 7 (bottom center right), 11 (right) © David Ball/Corbis; cover, title page (bottom left), p. 7 (bottom center left) © Lester Lefkowitz/Corbis; cover, title page (bottom right), pp. 7 (top left), 11 (left) © Arthur Tilley/Getty Images; p. 4 © Patrick Giardino/Corbis; p. 7 (top right) © Joseph Sohm, Visions of America/Corbis; p. 7 (bottom left) © Paul Gun/Corbis; p. 7 (bottom right) © Hubert Stadler/Corbis; p. 11 (center) © Digital Vision; p. 19 (top) © K. Hackenberg/zefa/Corbis; p. 19 (bottom) © www.istockphoto.com/Igor Karon.

Library of Congress Cataloging-in-Publication Data

Kravetz, Jonathan.
  Learning about energy with graphic organizers / Jonathan Kravetz.— 1st ed.
      p. cm. — (Graphic organizers in science)
  Includes index.
  ISBN 1-4042-3409-8 (library binding)
  1. Power resources—Juvenile literature. 2. Power resources—Charts, diagrams, etc.—Juvenile literature. I. Title. II. Series.
  TJ163.23.K73 2007
  333.79—dc22
                                        2005028984

Manufactured in the United States of America
CPSIA Compliance Information: Batch #CR017250PK: For Further Information Contact Rosen Publishing, New York, New York at 1-800-237-9932

Contents

Compare/Contrast Chart: Energy

	Potential Energy	Kinetic Energy
Diver	Standing on the diving board	Jumping from the board toward the water
Rubber Band	Pulling a rubber band	Letting the rubber band go
Waterfall	The water at the top of the fall	The falling water
Guitar String	Strings at rest	Plucking the string and causing it to vibrate, or move quickly

What Is Energy?

Energy is the ability to do work. Every time you lift a chair or walk to school, you use energy. When you eat a sandwich, your body gets energy. It changes the energy stored in the sandwich into energy for your body. Your body uses that energy to do work. The bus that drives you to school burns gasoline energy to do work. You are burning energy right now by reading this book!

The two basic types of energy are **potential energy** and **kinetic energy**. Potential energy is work that a thing might do. A rock sitting on top of a hill has potential energy because it could roll down the hill. Kinetic energy is moving energy. A rock rolling down the hill has kinetic energy because it is moving. Energy cannot be created or destroyed. Energy has always existed in one form or another.

This graphic organizer is called a compare/contrast chart. A compare/contrast chart allows you to compare the features of different things. The subjects are at the top of the columns. The features being compared are in the left column. This compare/contrast chart compares kinetic energy and potential energy.

Forms of Energy

Energy can come in many different forms. It can be changed from one type to another. The energy that lights our houses comes from electric energy. This is supplied by power plants that change **fossil fuels**, wind, water, or sunlight into electric energy.

Energy can also come directly from fossil fuels. Gasoline is an example of a fossil fuel. It provides energy for cars. Food is a source, or supply, of energy. Our bodies change food into energy. Plants change sunlight into energy they can use to grow.

Turn on a desk lamp or stand close to a fire. You will see light energy and feel heat energy. Do you hear the sound of a fly's wings? You can hear this because sound is carried through the air on **vibrations** called sound waves.

Concept webs are used to group facts about a subject. The subject goes in the middle, and the facts go around it. In this concept web, the subject is energy.

Concept Web: Energy

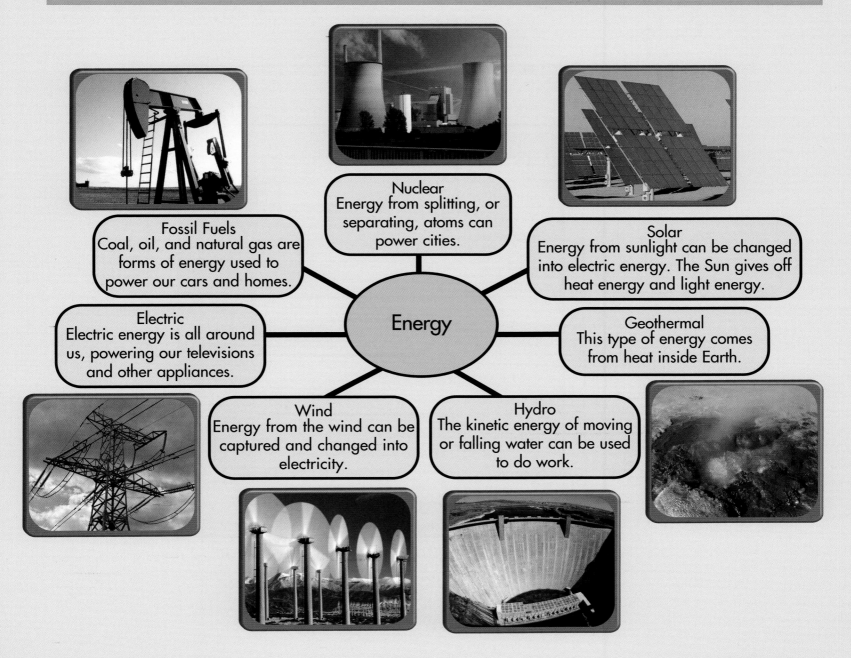

Nuclear
Energy from splitting, or separating, atoms can power cities.

Fossil Fuels
Coal, oil, and natural gas are forms of energy used to power our cars and homes.

Solar
Energy from sunlight can be changed into electric energy. The Sun gives off heat energy and light energy.

Electric
Electric energy is all around us, powering our televisions and other appliances.

Energy

Geothermal
This type of energy comes from heat inside Earth.

Wind
Energy from the wind can be captured and changed into electricity.

Hydro
The kinetic energy of moving or falling water can be used to do work.

Bar Graph: How Many Joules?

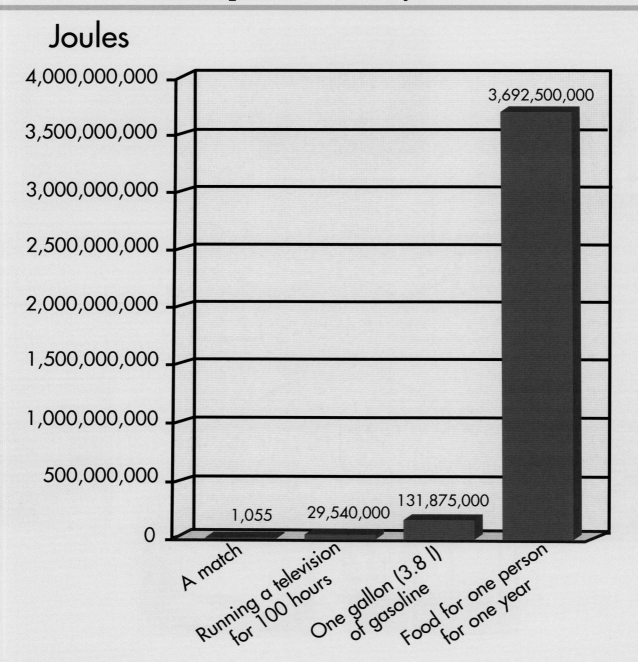

Joules

- 4,000,000,000
- 3,500,000,000
- 3,000,000,000
- 2,500,000,000
- 2,000,000,000
- 1,500,000,000
- 1,000,000,000
- 500,000,000
- 0

3,692,500,000

131,875,000

1,055   29,540,000

A match

Running a television for 100 hours

One gallon (3.8 l) of gasoline

Food for one person for one year

How Is Energy Measured?

Energy can be measured in a number of ways. Scientists measure energy in **joules**. Joules are named in honor of James Prescott Joule. He figured out that heat is a type of energy. A joule is the amount of energy needed to lift a 1 pound (.5 kg) object 9 inches (23 cm) off the ground. Shooting a basketball from the free-throw line takes about 15 joules. Throwing a fastball takes about 120 joules. Running a car for 5 minutes at 50 miles per hour equals about 373,737 joules. Other common ways people measure energy are the British Thermal Unit (BTU), the **volt**, and the **calorie**. BTUs are sometimes used when talking about heating systems. Volts are used to measure electricity. Calories are a measure of the amount of energy in food.

Bar graphs are used to compare things. In this bar graph, the amount of energy used or supplied by different things is compared.

Changing Energy

Energy cannot be created or destroyed, but it can be changed into other types of energy. This is the first law of **thermodynamics**. The food you eat has potential energy. After you eat it, your body changes it into energy so you can read, run, and talk. When your body uses that stored energy to do work, it becomes kinetic energy. The potential energy stored in a flashlight **battery** changes into light and heat energy when the flashlight is turned on. The gasoline in a car is stored energy that gets changed into kinetic energy when the car is started. Your television takes electric energy and changes it into light and sound.

The energy we use every day comes from many sources. These sources get changed when their potential energy is released, or let out.

A chart shows you how facts can be organized. This chart tells you how different types of energy are captured and used. It also shows you what percentage of the world's power it provides. A percentage is a part of the whole, or 100%.

Chart: Capturing Energy

Type of Energy Source	Energy Source	How Energy Is Captured	How Energy Is Released	Percentage of World Power
Fossil Fuels	Underground	Digging or drilling	Burning	80%
Nuclear Energy	Atoms	Nuclear reactors	Fusion/Fission	6.5%
Solar	Sun	Solar cells	Fusion releases heat and light	Trace
Wood	Forests	Cutting wood	Burning	10.8%
Hydropower	Water	Water running over dams	Water turns turbines	2.2%
Wind	Wind	Windmills	Wind turns turbines	Less than 1%

Flow Chart: Circuits

For a battery to light a lightbulb, the battery must be joined by an uninterrupted pathway. This pathway is called an electric circuit.

↓

The battery has two ends with opposite charges. The circuit starts at one end and ends at the other.

↓

The lightbulb will light up when the circuit is completed.

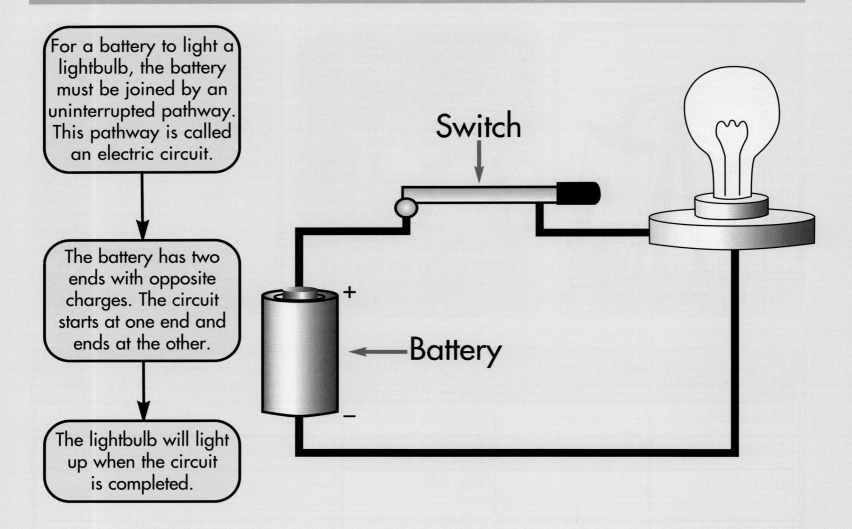

Switch

Battery

+

−

Electricity

Electricity is used to power lightbulbs, TV sets, computers, and many other household appliances. Electricity is easily changed into other forms of energy, such as heat and light. Electricity flows along wires, which makes it easy to conduct.

Electricity is caused by charged **particles**. All matter is made up of tiny particles called **atoms**. Atoms are made up of **protons**, **electrons**, and **neutrons**. Protons are positively charged and are drawn to electrons. Electrons have a negative charge. That is the charge opposite to that of protons. Neutrons have no charge. Protons and neutrons sit in the center of atoms in the **nucleus**. Electrons whiz around the nucleus. Electrons can move from one atom to another. When electrons move between atoms a current of electricity is created.

A flow chart is a group of pictures showing how something works. In this flow chart, we see a very simple electric circuit. On the left is a battery. Its energy lights the lightbulb.

Fossil Fuels

Fossil fuels are sources of potential energy that come from under the ground. There are three major types of fossil fuel. They are coal, oil, and natural gas. Fossil fuels were formed over hundreds of millions of years. They are nonrenewable. That means there is a limited amount of them.

Coal is a hard, black, rocklike matter. Coal is found in many places in the United States. Coal is mined, or dug out from the ground. Oil is a thick liquid. Natural gas is an odorless gas. To get oil and natural gas, companies drill into the earth. The oil and natural gas are then drawn up from below ground by machines. More than half of the oil we use comes from outside the United States. Most of it comes from the Middle East. The potential energy in fossil fuels is changed by burning it.

A pie chart compares amounts of the parts that make up a whole, or 100%. This pie chart shows the contents of one barrel of crude oil. That is what oil is called when it is first pumped out from under the ground. Crude oil is later made into different types of fuels at places called oil refineries. There are thousands of things that are made from oil.

Pie Graph: What Is in a Barrel of Oil?

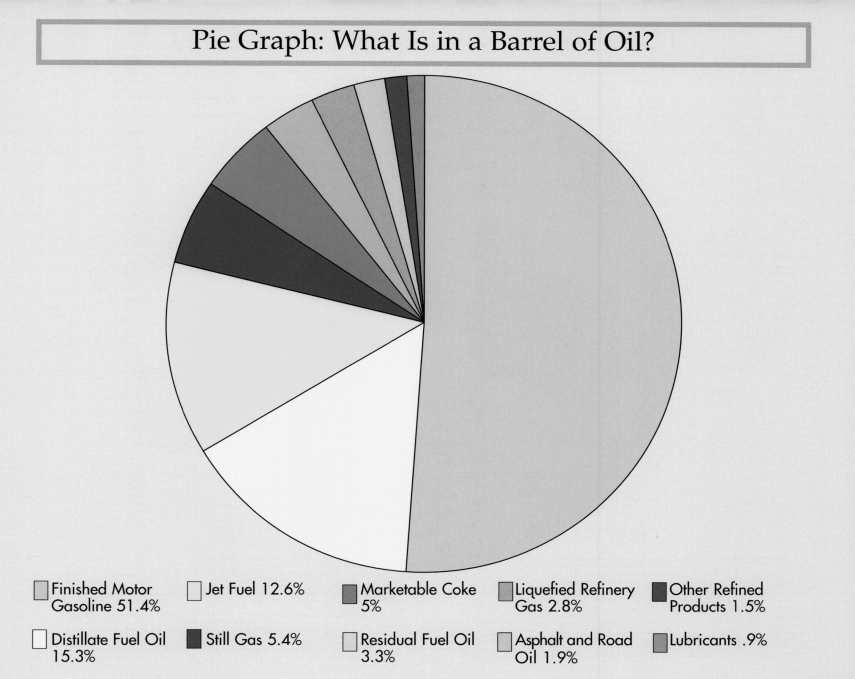

- Finished Motor Gasoline 51.4%
- Jet Fuel 12.6%
- Marketable Coke 5%
- Liquefied Refinery Gas 2.8%
- Other Refined Products 1.5%
- Distillate Fuel Oil 15.3%
- Still Gas 5.4%
- Residual Fuel Oil 3.3%
- Asphalt and Road Oil 1.9%
- Lubricants .9%

15

Cause-and-Effect Chart: Nuclear Fission

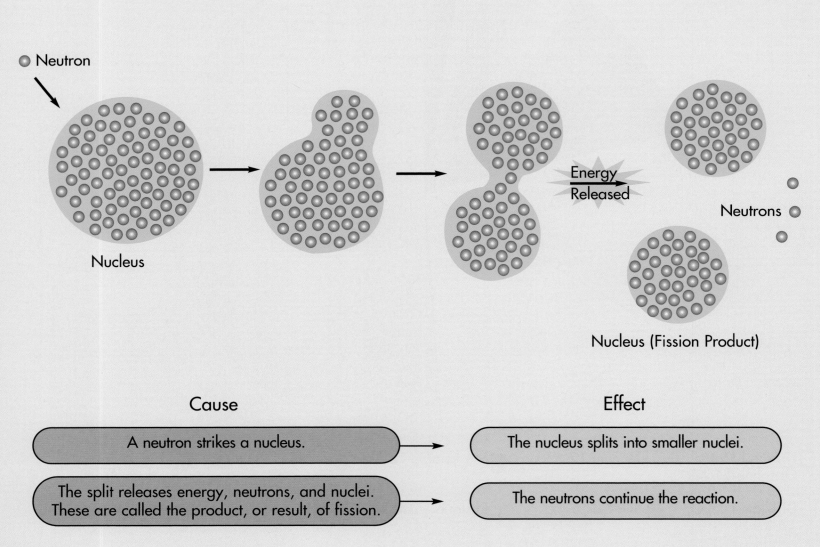

Neutron

Nucleus

Energy Released

Neutrons

Nucleus (Fission Product)

Cause

A neutron strikes a nucleus.

The split releases energy, neutrons, and nuclei. These are called the product, or result, of fission.

Effect

The nucleus splits into smaller nuclei.

The neutrons continue the reaction.

Nuclear Energy

Nuclear energy is the energy held inside atoms. Nuclear **reactions** release this energy from the **mass** of atoms. This mass energy is released in two ways. They are **fission** and **fusion**.

In nuclear fission the nuclei of atoms are split. This releases a lot of energy. This energy is used to produce electricity at a nuclear power plant. If the energy of a fission reaction is let out all at once, it can cause an explosion.

Another form of nuclear energy is called fusion. In nuclear fusion smaller nuclei are joined to make a larger nucleus. Nuclear fusion gives off a lot of heat and light. Scientists have tried to make a fusion **reactor** that produces electricity more efficiently. They keep trying because nuclear fusion creates less waste than fission. Also, its supply of fuel lasts longer.

A cause-and-effect chart lists causes on the left and effects on the right. Causes are things that happen. Effects are things that happen as a result of a cause. This chart explains nuclear fission.

Hydropower and Geothermal Energy

The kinetic energy of moving water can be used to do work. Moving water can be used to make electricity at hydroelectric plants. Hydroelectric energy is made from water power. Hydroelectric energy supplies about seven percent of the electricity used in the United States.

The heat of Earth is also a source of energy. It is called geothermal energy. "Geo" means "earth," and "thermal" means "heat." Hot water or steam from below ground can be used to make electricity using a geothermal power plant. Geothermal energy supplies about .4 percent of the electricity used in the United States. Hydro and geothermal energy are both renewable sources of energy. That means the supply of these fuels will not run out.

Sequence charts show the steps of something in order. This chart shows how a dam works.

Sequence Chart: How Does a Dam Work?

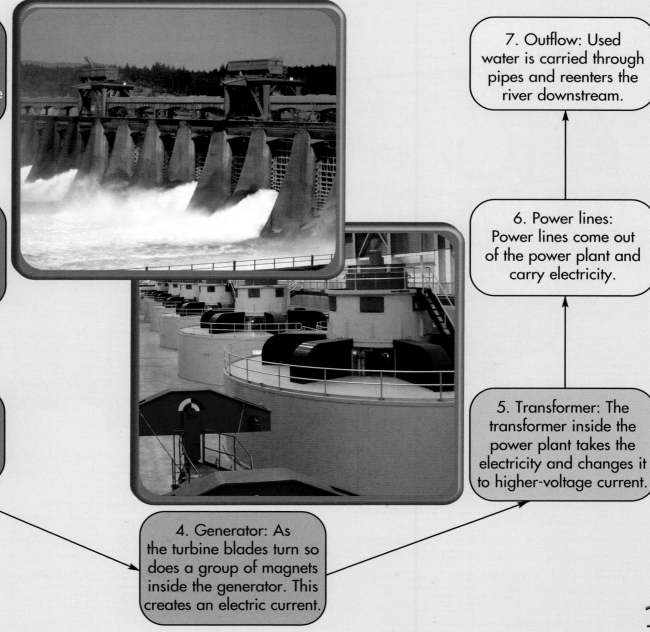

1. Dam: Most hydropower plants use a dam that holds back water. This creates a large pool of water.

2. Intake: Gates on the dam open and water falls through a pipe that leads to the turbine.

3. Turbine: The water turns the blades of a turbine, which is connected to a generator.

4. Generator: As the turbine blades turn so does a group of magnets inside the generator. This creates an electric current.

5. Transformer: The transformer inside the power plant takes the electricity and changes it to higher-voltage current.

6. Power lines: Power lines come out of the power plant and carry electricity.

7. Outflow: Used water is carried through pipes and reenters the river downstream.

19

Map: Wind Power

Power Class 1
Power Class 2
Power Class 3
Power Class 4
Power Class 5
Power Class 6
Power Class 7

Solar and Wind Energy

Energy from the Sun is called solar energy. It is made up of heat and light energy. We use the Sun's energy every day in many different ways. Solar energy can be used to produce electricity. It can also be used to heat water using special solar cells. Solar energy can only be gathered when the Sun is shining. The energy produced by the Sun can be stored and used later.

Wind can also be used to do work. The wind can be changed into other forms of energy, such as electric energy, which can then be stored. Farmers have been using wind energy for many years. They draw water from wells using windmills. Today wind is used to make electricity. One small windmill can power a home or a school.

This map shows the areas in the United States that are best suited for wind power. These areas are grouped in power classes numbered from 1 to 7, based on how strong the wind is in that area. Areas in power classes 4, 5, 6, and 7 are the best suited to use wind power.

Conservation

Only around seven percent of the world's energy comes from renewable energy sources. Most of our energy supply comes from fossil fuels. Fossil fuels take millions of years to form. Once they are used, they are gone forever. That's why it is important to conserve, or save, energy.

There are simple ways you can use less energy. You can turn off appliances and lights when you are not using them. You can recycle. It takes a lot of energy to make newspapers, plastic bottles, and other goods. Recycling means using these things again. They can be used to make new newspapers, bottles, and other goods.

There is another way people can help avoid running out of energy. It is to use more renewable energy sources, like solar power, wind power, and hydropower.

Glossary

atoms (A-temz) The smallest parts of elements that can exist either alone or with other elements.

battery (BA-tuh-ree) A thing in which energy is stored.

calorie (KA-luh-ree) An amount of food that the body uses to keep working.

electrons (ih-LEK-tronz) Particles inside atoms that spin around the nucleus. They have a negative charge.

fission (FIH-shun) The way a large nucleus is separated into two nuclei.

fossil fuels (FAH-sul FYOOLZ) Fuels, such as coal, natural gas, or gasoline, that were made from plants that died millions of years ago.

fusion (FYOO-zhun) The way two nuclei are joined together into one nucleus.

joules (JOOLZ) Standard measurements of energy.

kinetic energy (kuh-NEH-tik EH-nur-jee) Moving energy.

mass (MAS) The amount of matter in something.

neutrons (NOO-tronz) Particles with a neutral electric charge found in the nucleus of an atom.

nuclear (NOO-klee-ur) Having to do with the power created by splitting atoms, the smallest bits of matter.

nucleus (NOO-klee-us) Protons and neutrons joined together in the center of an atom.

particles (PAR-tih-kulz) Small pieces of something.

potential energy (puh-TEN-shul EH-nur-jee) Work that a thing might do.

protons (PROH-tonz) Particles with a positive electric charge found in the nucleus of an atom.

reactions (ree-AK-shunz) Releases of energy.

reactor (ree-AK-tur) The place in which nuclear reactions are carried out.

thermodynamics (ther-moh-dy-NA-miks) The study of the laws of changing energy from one form to another.

vibrations (vy-BRAY-shunz) Fast movements up and down or back and forth.

volt (VOHLT) A standard measurement of energy.

Index

Web Sites

Due to the changing nature of Internet links, PowerKids Press has developed an online list of Web sites related to the subject of this book. This site is updated regularly. Please use this link to access the list:
www.powerkidslinks.com/gosci/energy/